Julie An...

A Little Golden Book Biography

By Christy Webster

Illustrated by Sue Cornelison

A GOLDEN BOOK • NEW YORK

Text copyright © 2023 by Christy Webster
Cover art and interior illustrations copyright © 2023 by Sue Cornelison
All rights reserved. Published in the United States by Golden Books, an imprint of
Random House Children's Books, a division of Penguin Random House LLC, 1745 Broadway,
New York, NY 10019. Golden Books, A Golden Book, A Little Golden Book, the G colophon,
and the distinctive gold spine are registered trademarks of Penguin Random House LLC.
rhcbooks.com
Educators and librarians, for a variety of teaching tools, visit us at RHTeachersLibrarians.com
Library of Congress Control Number: 2022931976
ISBN 978-0-593-56419-6 (trade) — ISBN 978-0-593-56420-2 (ebook)
Printed in the United States of America
10 9 8 7 6 5 4 3 2 1

GW00854821

Julie Andrews was born Julia Elizabeth Wells on October 1, 1935, in a village called Walton-on-Thames, in England.

She grew up in a talented family. When she was a little girl, her aunt would help put on shows at a nearby playhouse. Julie's mother would play piano, and her father built sets.

Julie gave her very first performance at one of these shows. And she helped a fellow dancer whose hat had fallen over her eyes. Even at age three, Julie knew the show must go on!

When Julie was four years old, World War II began. At that point, Julie was living with her mother and stepfather in London, where bombs often fell.

To stay safe, Julie and her brother sometimes had to go to the countryside and live with strangers. While there, they loved learning to ride horses.

Other times, her family hid in the London Underground train stations with their neighbors. Her stepfather would play guitar to take people's minds off the danger.

Meanwhile, Julie was learning to dance and sing. She went to a special school, where she learned ballet and tap dance. At age nine, she started taking singing lessons.

Julie's mother was a wonderful piano player, and her stepfather was a well-known singer. They started to invite Julie onstage to sing with them. Julie enjoyed the spotlight.

Not long after the war finally ended, Julie was asked to perform for some British soldiers. She didn't know that Queen Elizabeth would also be in the audience! The queen told Julie that she sang beautifully.

Julie became known for her sweet, high voice. She spent her teenage years traveling around England, singing and dancing in shows. She loved the stage, but she missed her family when she was away.

Whenever she was homesick, Julie would go to her dressing room and read. Books helped her feel less lonely.

When Julie was sixteen years old, she went to see a musical on the West End of London, where some of the best plays in the world are performed.

Julie was amazed. The music! The costumes! The sets! She never thought she would have the chance to be in a show like that.

But she would—and soon! Just two years later, Julie was cast as the star in *Cinderella* on the West End. There were fancy costumes, a big moving set, and real ponies on the stage. Julie and the show got great reviews.

Thanks to the success of *Cinderella*,
Julie got her next big break—a role in a
Broadway musical, called *The Boy Friend*.
Julie was going to New York!

Julie was sad to leave, but she couldn't say no to Broadway. Her whole family gathered at the airport to see her off.

While rehearsing in New York, Julie struggled at first. Sometimes she felt she was doing a good job, and other times she didn't. The director told her to play the role as honestly as she could. On opening night, the audience gave the show a standing ovation.

The cast and crew waited overnight at a nearby restaurant to read the reviews in the next morning's newspaper. The critics loved the show—and Julie. It was official. Julie Andrews was a Broadway star!

Later that year, a songwriting duo named Lerner and Loewe were finishing their newest musical. They didn't think Julie would be available to star in it because most Broadway actors had two-year contracts. But Julie had only wanted a one-year contract for her first show so that she could visit her family sooner.

After a quick trip to England, Julie went back to New York to star in *My Fair Lady*.

Julie played a flower seller named Eliza Doolittle who learns to speak like a fancy lady. Just like Eliza, Julie had to learn to speak in a new accent. It was very difficult.

Her hard work paid off. *My Fair Lady* became the longest-running Broadway musical at the time, and the cast recording was the number-one album of 1956.

Julie continued to act and sing in hit musicals. One day, Walt Disney visited her backstage after a show. He wanted her to star in his next movie. Julie had performed on Broadway, at the famous Carnegie Hall, and on television—but never in movies.

By then, Julie had gotten married. Not long after giving birth to her first daughter, Julie and her family flew to Hollywood, California, so Julie could star in Walt Disney's *Mary Poppins*. Julie won the Academy Award for Best Actress for her performance as the magical nanny—and fans everywhere learned the word "supercalifragilisticexpialidocious."

In 1965, just one year after *Mary Poppins* was released, Julie starred in *The Sound of Music*. In this movie musical, Julie played a nun in training named Maria who falls in love while looking after seven children in the Austrian mountains. It became one of her most famous roles, thanks to such songs as "My Favorite Things" and "Do-Re-Mi."

Julie spent the next twenty years starring in movies. She also welcomed four more children into her life.

One day, Julie's stepdaughter, Jenny, asked her to write a story for her. That was when Julie came up with the idea for her first children's book. She would go on to write and publish many more.

Thirty-five years after leaving New York to make *Mary Poppins*, Julie finally decided to return to Broadway. She brought her role from the movie musical *Victor/Victoria* to the stage.

Julie worked as hard as ever on this show, and it was a big success.

Over the years, Julie sometimes found that her voice got very tired, especially after singing in a Broadway show for many months in a row. She had to take long rests, do special exercises, and occasionally have surgery to help keep her voice healthy. But at one point, something went wrong. After her most recent surgery, she found that she couldn't sing at all.

Julie was sad—she loved to sing! But although fifty years had passed since she had read alone in her dressing room, she knew books could still bring comfort in a difficult time. With the help of her daughter Emma, Julie wrote and published many more children's books and books about her own life.

Julie stayed busy. She helped others, spent
time with her family, and kept starring in films.
She played a queen in the *Princess Diaries* movies
and another queen in the *Shrek* movies. But she
said it was the greatest honor of her life when
the real queen—Queen Elizabeth II—gave her
a special award honoring her work.

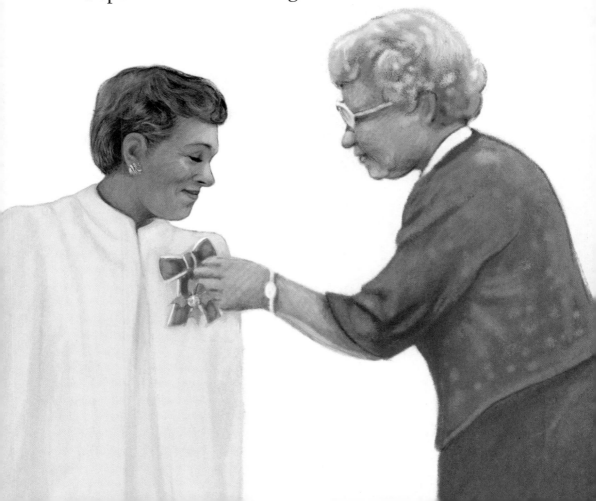

Julie Andrews followed her dreams, going from her small village to London, New York, Hollywood, and all over the world. She worked hard to create unforgettable characters on the screen, in books, and onstage.

Her many fans will always be inspired by her talents, and they will always love Julie Andrews.